Gale

July 30, th 2001

Looie's Birchday = 67

Max Dupain's
Australia

Max Dupain's
Australia

VIKING

For my grandchildren
Erin and Lauren.
May they love life
and live long.

Viking
Penguin Books Australia Ltd
487 Maroondah Highway, P.O. Box 257
Ringwood, Victoria, 3134, Australia
Penguin Books Ltd
Harmondsworth, Middlesex, England
Viking Penguin Inc.,
40 West 23rd Street, New York, N.Y. 10010, U.S.A.
Penguin Books Canada Limited,
2801 John Street, Markham, Ontario, Canada, L3R 1B4
Penguin Books (N.Z.) Ltd,
182–190 Wairau Road, Auckland 10, New Zealand

First published 1986 by Viking

Reprinted 1988

Created and produced by
Mead & Beckett Publishing
139 Macquarie Street, Sydney N.S.W. 2000, Australia

Designed by Leonie Bremer-Kamp
Edited by Amanda Bilson
Typeset in Hong Kong by Asco Trade Typesetting Limited
Photographs prepared in Hong Kong by Bright Arts
Made and printed in Hong Kong by Leefung-Asco Printers

National Library of Australia
Cataloguing in Publication data

Dupain, Max, 1911–

Max Dupain's Australia

ISBN 0 670 81525 X

1. Photography—Australian   2. Australia—Description
and travel.   3. Australia—description and travel—views.
4. Australia—Social life and customs—20th century.
5. Australia—Social life and customs—20th century—Pictorial
works.   I. Title.

994.04

SUNDAY MORNING ON THE CLARENCE RIVER, CIRCA 1960s
*Page 1: A pleasant break for the photographer, having spent
several days on an arduous industrial assignment at the CSR
sugar mills in the region. Forecast, clear and sunny.*

STREET SCENE, CIRCA 1960s
*Page 2: Newsboy discovers sex, providing he has turned to the
right page. Judging by his expression he has—and he's
disappointed!*

CONTENTS

PAST IMPERFECT *by Max Dupain*

THIS COLLECTION of pictures is not intended to be a tourist's guide to the halcyon escape routes of Australia. It is, instead, a very personal distillation of places and events I have encountered with 50-odd years of practising my craft in my own country. Regard it as a broad cross-section of intimate visual relationships which hopefully will afford pleasure, richness, some inner knowledge and maybe even joy and humour.

Much of my work has the blessing of recording history, with a large dose of nostalgia thrown in for its soothing effect. Occasionally, a unique subject crops up, like 'Roadsign, Queensland', the cow's skull on the post warning reckless drivers of the dangers lurking in the treacherous bends. Where else in the world would you see the like? 'The Queen, 1954' series conveys the essence of a passive mob indulging in the enjoyment of its 'circus'. The faces explain everything.

The old tram pictures in the city are reminiscent of discomfort and danger. Sometimes, if you just missed a tram, you could race after it, grab the side handles and haul yourself aboard! Or, if you failed to pull the stop signal when approaching your destination and the tram passed the stop at a reasonable amble, you could always take a leap, hit the road with the offside foot and end up in the gutter, mostly right side up. You had to be young!

'Nuns at Newport Beach' is tinged with a slightly surreal quality, and I considered myself lucky to come across this scene while sunbaking on the beach with my faithful old Rolleiflex close to the chest. Photography needs a lot of luck, as is also demonstrated in 'Meat queue'. But the viewer will not find any shockers in the form of photographs depicting heroic adventures, melodramatic actions or situations where the power of human survival is pushed beyond its normal limits. Moments of agony are out.

In fact, looking back on so much work, I have to admit there is a certain serenity, a kind of emotional intensity, which probably reflects the rather wonderful life I have enjoyed as an Australian, here in Australia. No one could be more thankful.

The embryo days of my own studio life began in 1934, after five undistinguished years (apart from the rowing!) at Sydney Grammar School, thanks to the generosity of my parents, and an immediate apprenticeship with Cecil Bostock lasting three years. My studio consisted of a single room and a processing room up the passage which I shared with a photographer called Harold Venn. The address was 24 Bond Street. These were days when you could park your car in the street, unlocked, all day and all night and only get booked if you were dead unlucky. Nothing would be stolen. I didn't acquire a car until 1936. It was an open Chevrolet Roadster and became known locally as 'The Yellow Terror'.

At about this time I moved to larger premises on the fifth floor of the same building to facilitate a growing practice. The new studio had large, box-framed windows facing east. These could be opened at any time in the summer months to let through great gusts of north-easterly wind, bringing its sweet-salty tang. This building long ago gave way to an air conditioned filing cabinet for office workers. It is now sealed off against the north-easter as well as against the stench of gasoline fumes. This was the time that Aldous Huxley was saying, 'Civilisation is Sterilisation'!

A third photographer inhabited 24 Bond Street, Reg Johnson. He was well established and we became close friends. I shall be forever grateful for his critical appraisal of my work and enthusiastic encouragement. Reg was a strong character, self taught and with a ton of vitality. He had a large studio fitted out with the latest equipment in lighting devices, cameras, lenses, enlargers etc. It must be remembered that at this time, artifical light photography had only recently been born. The beautiful south light windows of the old studio were giving way to electric light as a matter of speed, consistency and convenience. Soft daylight has been rediscovered since, and for a lot of studio work it is still invaluable. Johnson was devoted to the studio operation and eventually relinquished location work. He manoeuvred it in my direction and I readily accepted, irrespective of what it consisted of or the location.

Before I had 'The Yellow Terror', trams were my main means of transport. The gear used to be stored

---

NUNS AT NEWPORT BEACH, 1960
The incongruity of this picture is its essence. A lucky group movement, and the significance of the hands adds to the picture's overall surreal quality.

in the rear control compartment and if the conductor was at all genial, I was allowed to stand there with it. If he was not, I had to sit on the nearest available wooden bench and forever have my eyes over my shoulder, just in case. 'One 3d ticket to Market Street, please!' CSR, who is my oldest client, would occasionally ask me to photograph a piece of new equipment at Pyrmont. Imagine hawking the gear from Bond Street to Pyrmont by tram. If I remember rightly, you boarded the tram at Pitt Street which took you to Market Street and there you had to change onto a west-bound tram, cross the old Pyrmont Bridge and eventually end up at the end of Harris Street at the CSR refinery. Today, that sort of travel time would cost more than the job was worth.

Equipment in Australia was scarce, especially cameras. My own totally versatile Thornton Pickard Half Plate, given to me by my father as a starting off present, was a beautiful, handmade timber camera with double dark slides made for housing glass plates, which preceeded the cut film system. It weighed a ton. Due to so much location work at that time, my right biceps is now larger than my left!

Johnson was a technical perfectionist, the camera to him was sacrosanct. His philosophy was American-oriented and he achieved marvellously the sheer 'quality' demonstrated in American work at the time. To me, with my one wooden wonder, climbing the slow ladder of success, this was fascinating. He worked in 20 × 25 cm (8 × 10 in) ultimately, and his concerns were illustrative—pretty girls and more pretty girls. There was no choice if you were going to pay the rent. To try and make a 20 × 25 cm (8 × 10 in) camera operate economically it was necessary to cut down on film consumption. So the night before a big job, Johnson would go to bed (in the studio) and work out his model positioning, his lighting system, viewpoint and lens potential. When the action started it was more or less a matter of organising everything into his preconceived pattern and taking the picture—no

MEAT QUEUE, 1946
Queuing at a Sydney butcher's just after the war. It is an interesting shot because of the consistent ages of the subjects and also because at the decisive moment of exposure, the middle figure decided to break from the queue. This created a movement in her neighbour which centralised the action.

waste. The bemused and bewildered client would be handed one beautiful 20 × 25 cm (8 × 10 in) contact print instead of the normal six or so 12.5 × 10 cm (5 × 4 in). No selection—that's it mate!

I admired Johnson's photographic integrity which produced such beautiful pictures. They tragically lost 50 per cent of their quality and tonal range in the crude reproduction methods of the period. He ultimately gave it all up and pursued medical motion picture photography for which he always had a leaning. He did some brilliant work in Australia which he took to the States. Not without downright persistence was he able to show his work to a large group of eminent surgeons who were indeed impressed. He returned to Australia with an Honorary Doctorate in Medicine.

Early pictures were referred to as 'snapshots'. I think it was part of a trade gimmick invented by Kodak who started the amateur market and clinched it with the slogan, 'You press the button—we do the rest'. They are still doing it! 'Shots' is the current derivative which originated in America, along with the expression 'taking pictures'. 'Shots' has a shutter connotation and is synonymous with the trigger of a gun. The evolution of the camera follows that of the gun, or runs parallel with it. Firstly, the slow hand-loaded muzzle gun, then the firing piece with the factory-made bullet to shoot faster; the bullet clips with a quantity of missiles to fire under pressure of spring loading; the sub-machine gun and fully automated weapons all represent a parallel history of change and development.

The camera shutter is the counterpart. It has been the subject of unique design changes and development and is the focal point of the 'gun' analogy. First there was no shutter at all, just a lens with a cap which the operator removed and replaced after an interval of time, thereby providing adequate exposure for the slow-rated film of the time. Then came the roller blind shutter which consisted of a horizontal slot in a strip of strong fabric rolled into a spring-loaded shaft. The setting was achieved by pulling a cord with a red pom pom on the end. This wound up together the spring and the slotted fabric. A ratchet stopped the spring unwinding until the release was touched, then the slot flicked past the lens giving the required exposure. A great clatter accompanied this. It was the forerunner of the focal plane shutter.

I remember using a flap shutter attached to a huge Adams Studio camera in the Bond Street studio. It was worked by air pressure against a piston in a small cylinder. The pressure was built up by squeezing a bulb attached to a rubber tube fitted to the cylinder through a hole in the wooden lens panel. The bulb had a hole in its end over which the photographer put his thumb to contain the air and then squeezed, holding the squeeze for as long as the exposure demanded, and then letting go. All very inaccurate, but it symbolised the mechanical beginnings of photographic equipment.

Once, on a visit to Australia in the 1930s, George Hoyningen-Huene, the top fashion photographer for *Harper's Bazaar*, was using my studio for a fashion assignment. He could not get the hang of the bulb-squeezing system, particularly the thumb covering the hole. So we improvised with a wooden plug and inserted it into the hole. Of course the inevitable happened—when the bulb was squeezed hard, the plug flew out and whacked the fashion director in the ear! Great laughter all round.

After the flap, the focal plane shutter took over. For many years it proved to be the best of all and is still used, although highly refined, in the manufacture of 35mm cameras. It has wonderful accuracy, an even coverage of the film area from edge to edge and operates in close proximity to the film surface. Along with this was developed the compur shutter, a multi-blade instrument which opens from the centre to the periphery and closes again, thereby giving minuscule over-exposure in the centre. But this can now be harnessed, together with the focal plane shutter, to a battery-operated monster, not unlike a machine gun, which you point at the subject, follow if necessary, let rip at three single exposures and rewind per second at any shutter speed above a 15th of a second. Today, a subject does not have to be studied and personally directed. The photographer machine guns every gesture, movement and facial expression. From the ensuing map of images, there *has* to be one which fulfils the client's requirements. Does this signify the end of yet another human element in photography? Leave aside personal, sensitive judgement and objec-

CHRISTMAS HOLIDAYS, NARRABEEN, NSW, 1938
Two things the average Australian loves to indulge in are camping and fishing. This sight is ideal for both—camping on flat land and fishing in either the still lake or the sea. Today, this area is still a campsite, but caravans have replaced the tents.

tify everybody and everything. For God's sake, let's keep individuality out of this!

Before describing further the technical crudities of the early 1930s and passing into more esoteric stuff, I will relate a short anecdote about the generation of light, which might raise a laugh. There was no mobile electronic flash gear in those days, not even a flashbulb, but there was this demonic device called flash powder. While working with Bostock, the old devil sent me out single-handed to photograph a dinner somewhere in the Western Suburbs. By the time I got there the guests were finishing the main course and about to hoe into the desserts. I set up the camera on an elevated podium at the end of the room and began to make ready the flash equipment. The powder consisted of grey magnesium mixed with minute particles of clay to weigh it down. It had to be spread out on an angled pan about 30 cm (12 in) long to which was attached a stick so that it could be held aloft. A piece of paper like a wide flat wick was slipped in before it was hoisted up. All set to go, with the photographer trembling violently from head to foot. Camera ready, lens stopped down, shutter set on 'time', slide drawn, let her rip: open shutter, strike match, hold pan well up behind camera, reach for the touch paper with the lit match and within a fraction of a second a muffled roar hit the room. Audible shock rent the air! Close shutter, close slide, withdraw same, pack up quick and then withdraw yourself with gear before the pale white cloud now hanging on the whole ceiling finally settles into the strawberries and cream, lemon chiffon pie and ice cream, and crème de menthe marshmallow. It sounds funny now, but then—phew!

I hold the Bond Street operation exceptionally dear. They were days of vital beginnings for my photography punctuated by unforgettable events, such as the rediscovery of solarisation; the portraits of famous conductors and musicians made possible through the promotion of Beryl Ross of the ABC; the new flexibilities of double printing; the discovery of Man Ray and the radical thinking of his Dada confederates; the sheer professionalism of Edward Steichen; the new work being done overseas and its arrival on our doorstep in magazine form—photographic revelations by Horst, Muncaszi, George Hoyningen-Huene, Toni Frizell, de Meyer, Louise Dahl Wolf, Bill Brandt, Brassai, the adventurous Margaret Burke White and hordes of others. This was all shared by the interesting people I had around me including my first wife Olive,

who only recently put up a memorable retrospective exhibition; Geoff Powell, a forthright individual who would insist on growing a beard in a society not beard oriented. Geoff fell heavily for the Russian Ballet in 1938 and spent many extra curricular hours at rehearsals getting unique pictures. I remember him returning to the studio late one evening and bursting in on a small group of us, drinking coffee and arguing. He had made a feverish return from the theatre for film replenishment. In his breathless haste he had only one comment to make: 'I'm up in the flys!' before grabbing new stock and flying out again followed by much friendly laughter and banter. Great days!

There was also Damien Parer with whom I had much in common, although I did not share his devout religious beliefs. But he was so thoroughly integrated with his faith that one did not question his deep-seated philosophy. He was obsessed with motion picture photography and the work he did in the studio, though competently executed, was fill-in stuff between the few movie assignments he was offered. He brought new thinking and photographic awareness to the studio. The words 'documentary' and 'factual' were being bandied about in the late 1930s and Damien would sound off at every opportunity about Robert Flaherty, Grierson and Lorenz, protagonists of the new theory and practice. His favourite quote was Grierson's assessment of the photographic document: 'The creative treatment of actuality'. It still rings in my ears. I'd be very content to say that Damien was the most lovable and sincere person I have known; he was totally honest and delightfully naïve. He was also critical of his own work far beyond reasonable judgement. The war, with tragic irony, gave him his great opportunity and he joined the Department of Information camera team. They kicked off in the Middle East under Frank Hurley but in no time were back in Australia preparing fearlessly for a probe with the 21st Brigade into New Guinea. There he made some of the most dramatic, authentic and human documentaries of the whole war: *Assault in Salamoa*, *Kokoda Trail* and *Battle of the Bismarck Sea*. This last was done from Beaufighter aircraft (the Japs called them 'whispering death'), flown by Torchy Uren. We had several foregatherings after that but Damien fell to the Japanese in the Central Pacific. He had accepted a post with US forces and was sent to Peleliu Island where he was killed in action.

Even in remote Australia the war was in every-

MOSMAN BAY, SYDNEY, 1946
This is an early morning lucky shot, with the Mosman ferry approaching the wharf for the commuter pick-up. Atmospherically, I find it reminiscent of the pictorial school of the 1920s, the only difference being that it's sharper!

body's life, but I rather scorned the heroics of it all and despised the negativism created by brute force. I was a pacifist and became interested in a new wartime venture sponsored by Professor Dakin of the Department of Marine Biology at the University of Sydney. With knowledge of the survival reflexes of the animal and marine kingdom he began to apply these principles to the soldier in warfare. Some contempt and even scorn was heaped upon him by the brass until, in the initial stages of a skirmish in New Guinea, Australian conscripts were massacred in a single encounter. These soldiers had been issued with standard khaki uniforms and were fighting in the bright green vegetation of the tropics. They stood out like dogs' balls on a cold night. Dakin let them have it good. He roasted the brass in the press and elsewhere. Regrettably, television did not exist! Eventually camouflage became officially established in both army and airforce.

Just prior to this, I was approached by an old friend and preparatory school comrade to consider the amalgamation of our then mutual photographic operations. Ernest Hyde was a younger member of Hartland & Hyde who were the leading process engravers in Australia at the time. It was early 1941, and Hartland & Hyde were inducing the painful birth of colour photography in Sydney. It should have been a Caesarean, but instead it laboured on until natural resources dried up and a still birth seemed imminent. I was asked to apply whatever life-giving support I could and breathe fresh energy into the ailing infant. I accepted Ernest's offer and moved to 49 Clarence Street. It was a new venture but destined temporarily to a short life. The war claimed Ernest who went off to Canada to train with the RAAF. He eventually became a navigator in Bomber Command and was away from Australia for three years.

Olive Cotton, who had resigned from the studio after our marriage broke up, was invited to take over the photographic operations until such time as we both, hopefully, returned from our respective war occupations. Both Ernest and I were grateful to Olive for accepting the post.

I, meanwhile, had already joined up with Dakin's team and was put to work in a training school at

ROADSIGN, QUEENSLAND, CIRCA 1970s
The sardonic Australian sense of humour is seen here embellishing a roadsign, cobwebs and all.

Bankstown aerodrome, in preparation for a stint in Darwin as an accredited camouflage officer to the RAAF. The war caused a gigantic upheaval. Before long I was on my way to Darwin with a camouflage confederate, Gus Dignam. We took a train to Adelaide and stayed there for several days awaiting the arrival of a utility vehicle which we were taking to Darwin. We had to have it lashed to a flat bed rail truck and hauled by the 'Gahn' to Alice Springs which was the end of the rail line as well as the end of the earth! From there we were to drive it to Darwin, 900 miles up the new military road known as the Stuart Highway. Professor Dakin was to be our passenger from Alice. We virtually lived in that van for three days and three nights en route to Alice. Canned food was the staple diet: bully beef, meat and veg, prunes and rice and more bully beef. The cans were passed to the engine driver who warmed them up on an engine hot plate designed for such contingencies. Sleep was spasmodic; when the sun set the heat vanished like a material presence and we froze until dawn. I can remember dozing off at night surrounded by the gibber plains of the Stuart Desert lit by the blazing starlight of the interior. We travelled all night and woke up the next morning to exactly the same spectacle as the previous evening. We stopped for water and a change of drivers at various refurbishing points along the way. We also stretched aching limbs at previously unheard of places—Banka Banka, Powell Creek, Birdum Creek, Mataranka, Burrindie, to name but a few.

Dakin was late by about ten days so Gus and I took the van and explored the haunting landscape of the MacDonnell Ranges. Standley Chasm and Simpsons Gap were unforgettable sights for which, as coastal inhabitants, we were totally unprepared. Great rearing cliffs of red granite arching into pure cobalt, and white-trunked eucalypts sprouting from their flanks. It was like grand drama of the highest order, and of course I photographed it thoroughly before a reluctant departure. Compared with life on the 'Gahn', we experienced more comfort at the staging camps up the highway, but eventually arrived at Darwin a somewhat scruffy, tangled and deadbeat trio.

I had not counted on being in Darwin for nearly a year designing and building camouflage screens to cover new oil tank installations. A lot of the storage tanks had been destroyed by Japanese bombing the previous year. The town had been wrecked, the landscape was flat and dull, and the heat and humidity unbearable. It was a patched-up military town and fortunately for the sanity of all, a little skullduggery provided beer in plenty. We built camouflage and photographed it for southbound reports—evidence of progress in technique and proof that our lives were not being totally wasted. But it was all too late; the Japs were on the run and another raid on Darwin was a remote possibility. Only twice did the sirens wail at midnight and the personnel scuttle into slit trenches. The wheels of bureaucracy had been turning too long for a sudden cessation of activities.

One day, out of the blue, came an order to the C.O. from Professor Dakin: 'Instruct Dupain return Sydney first available flight, short leave prior photographic work in N.G. area.' Dated 25.1.44. It turned out I was to research and report on camouflage work being done in New Guinea by both the Yanks and the Aussies. I flew to Goodenough Island where the camouflage HQs were housed and met up with my old mate from early Bankstown days, Robert Emerson Curtis, who was commanding officer of operations in the area. I spent four months in New Guinea mainly contacting the Yanks, learning their evaluation of camouflage and how it was applied. They were almost over-cooperative and would sometimes leave a job for the express purpose of discussing a point with me. Or they would take me to sites where camouflage was being applied and press written information on me. I followed the American operation from Goodenough Island to the Admiralty Islands and New Britain. At this stage of the war, camouflage was being phased out. The Yanks were not terribly worried about concealment of tanks, airplanes, guns etc. of which they had endless supplies—they figured the more the Japs saw of this vast mountain of weaponry the better! It rolled along the roads of Finschhafen day and night. They were preparing for the assault on Aitape.

On returning to Sydney I put in my resignation to the Department of Home Security and applied to the Department of Information for a job as a war photographer. Maslin Williams (great friend of Parer's and director of motion picture photography in the DOI) heard the news and suggested that we forget the war, which was now on its last legs, and prepare for the future, particularly in regard to the immigration issue which loomed pretty large on the labour platform at the time. Through Williams' influence I was offered a job covering as much of Australia's way of life as possible for overseas publicity. My work was to be directed at potential migrants. I took it on and visited all the capital cities and environs except Darwin! I hope the thousands of negatives I made, all with a Rolleiflex, are preserved in archival conditions in the department's stores. They would now require an historical classification.

I dearly wanted to return to the studio and start a civilised life again. The unstable wartime years, the grudging adaptation to ever-changing surroundings, the thousands of impressions both good and bad of varying environments, all added up to long-term shock. I just needed a settled emotional life for a while in order to get my life and work into a new perspective. I did not want to go back to the 'cosmetic lie' of fashion photography or advertising illustration. I had seen too much of another kind of reality which probed deeper and demanded uneqivocal attention—or else.

I married again—her name, Diana Illingworth. She had been deeply entrenched by proxy in my life during the war, and now the time was right for us to team up and bear some fruit. Daughter and son ripened on the vine in that order. They changed the rules and made all the choices and to this day they still do—somewhat! All in all I would never have wanted or asked for more satisfaction, but I do ask myself, have I reciprocated adequately?

I always had a hankering for architecture. In my youth I made drawings from reproductions of Greek temples and capitals, and later in school my interest in the practical application of materials to structural purposes made me think seriously about becoming an architect. But mathematics and physics were my undoing. I was thrown at any attempt to understand either. Even today, the logic of it all is shrouded in a mist. Architecture was discounted on a technicality! But eventually there developed another way of getting involved—through photography, and my interest was intense enough to practise and promote this specialised field in the 1950s. I was encouraged by architects Samuel Lipson (my first client), John D. Moore, Walter Bunning and later by Syd Ancher and Arthur Baldwinson.

My associates at the time and I practised architectural photography for over 30 years almost as a full-time occupation, and I consider some of my best work has been produced in the area of architecture. At the beginning of this involvement more talented people joined the studio. David Moore stayed for a num-

MAIN SHELLS, SYDNEY OPERA HOUSE, CIRCA 1970s
The last of the tile-laying on the gigantic shells of the Opera House. Lucky for the photographer to have scale and human interest in such strategic point in the composition.

ber of years and worked hard and consistently. He had also been interested in architecture as a profession but was seduced and ultimately captivated by the camera. He travelled overseas for seven years to see the world and be a photo journalist. He worked successfully for the magazines of the time, and celebrated his return to Sydney with a stimulating exhibition at the Macquarie Gallery called 'Seven years a stranger'. David is one of the few photographers I know with whom I can enjoy good conversation about photography and its relationship to life. I enjoyed the quiet persistence and pleasant personality of Kerry Dundas who also became interested in studio activities. Like most photographers who do a lot of routine work, Kerry spent a great deal of time and energy making pictures for exhibitions, the heart-soul products made spontaneously and outside the jurisdiction of 'the client'. Kerry departed from the studio to take over the photography department of the Art Gallery of New South Wales. Many other photographers passed through the studio on their way towards every photographer's dream—to have his own equipment and be able to do his own thing when and how he likes. Of course this dream is never completely realised; it remains largely a figment of the imagination, in reality frustrated by the whims and indecisions of clients, deadlines, weather, finance, outside laboratories, plus one's own physical and mental limitations.

In order to preserve the personal touch, I have always wanted to work with a small staff. Photography, the way I want to do it, is entirely dependent on the idiosyncracies of the individual. Mass-produced photography may be more lucrative, but at the same time it's a god-awful bore. I have found that if the photographers in my studio perform the full operation—liaison with the client, exposing film, processing that film, selecting top shots from the run, making proofs and final prints, then complete commitment and satisfaction is experienced. There is no dependence on other peoples' interpretations. Once the quality of the negatives has been proven in the enlargers, repeat printing can always be performed by others who are sympatico with the job.

Today, my studio operates with only three full-time people. Apart from myself there is Jill White, who has been closely involved for twenty years, on and off, (the 'off' being when she married and went to live in Fiji for a while). Apart from developing her uniquely personal child and portrait photography, she knows all

there is to know about keeping a studio on the move—and does! I often say to myself (and out loud!) 'If she goes we might as well all follow!' Tom Balfour is indigenous to South Australia. He spent six years freelancing in architectural photography and decided to expand his talents in Sydney. He has been practising successfully in the Artarmon studio for over two years. Quite often one hears of graduates in architecture disavowing their academic qualifications and applying their talents to photography. Tom is different in so far as he graduated in law before surrendering, and law was preceded by two years studying architecture. I am inclined to spit upon the academy, probably due to my own inability to come to terms with the studious life. In Tom's case I hesitate, confounded by his formidable background. With a small working family like ours, thoughts and actions are so integrated that there has to be harmony. Lots of problems, whether ethical, practical or personal, are solved by discussion. Mutual interest in all the work being produced is mandatory, and constructive, critical comments are forever forthcoming. Also humour and good cheer are plentiful, and I find this very special workshop a happy place to spend most of my working days. I truly believe this sentiment is shared by all of us.

One vital activity which is often overlooked is the studio's dependence on our holding company, Hartland & Hyde Activities. Their management of financial affairs, sales tax returns and all the sordid details which accompany any business is a veritable weight off our minds.

Looking back on my experiences and the philosophy they determined for me, I have to acknowledge my indebtedness to many people. Ure Smith for one, whose altruistic spirit towards all things relating to art helped me find myself and my direction in photography. Likewise his confederate, Leon Gellert, poet and author, who was partly instrumental in bringing my career to life.

The words of basic art wisdom which emanated from Henry Gibbons at Julian Ashton's Art School still mean so much to me: 'It is all a matter of form and movement'. This elemental principal, a comment

SHEARERS, WESTERN QUEENSLAND, 1978
Working the land is hard yakka and the shearer does more than his bit. It is back breaking work day in, day out—for the young and fit only.

on my crude drawing of a plaster cast of a hand or a head, explained so much and cleared the air for greater understanding. Today, when I make a photograph, be it architectural, still life, portrait, or anything which has to be considered and not shot on the run, Gibbons' maxims still precede any action of mine.

Then there was Cecil Bostock, so often irreconcilable; loved one day and hated the next. I joined him immediately after school which was towards the end of the Depression. He could barely afford to hire me because work in the early 1930s was hardly plentiful. Bostock was a foundation member of the Sydney Camera Circle which, despite its fixation with the English Pictorial School, did have an idealistic philosophy by today's standards. It was elitist. Bostock and Cazneaux were thought of as the exponents of upper-crust photography in Australia. The former objective in approach and finish; the latter subjective in attitude and content. Bostock was versatile and had unquestionable technical ability, Cazneaux was a romantic, in love with life. It was my good fortune to be able to cope with Bostock's mechanical thoroughness and pragmatism; these elements helped straighten out my romantic schoolboy notions. I was very conscious of his methods and simple principles which aimed at perfection at any price within human limits. He loved good craftmanship and apart from being photographically oriented, he was a capable commercial artist, a master bookbinder and, for a hobby, he built himself a powerboat. He did not write poetry, neither was he a literary buff nor a lover of fine music. I doubt whether he knew one good wine from another!

In my youth I was in awe of the power of Michelangelo, the dramatic light of Rembrandt and the serene earthiness of Constable. But I grew up with the Impressionists, read about them and devoured reproductions of their work. It was not until 1978 when I visited the Jeu de Paume in Paris that the full impact of their achievement struck home, with poignant revelations about the divinity of light on which all photography is dependent.

There is only a handful of beloved artists whose work illuminates the little scenario of my life's endeavours in photography. Great creative minds whose works I hold so dearly to be the finest of all man's gifts to civilisation. My list is polyglot: philosophers, novelists, poets and composers. Beethoven, whose clarity of thought and execution I have loved and sworn by and in a humble way endeavoured to emulate in my own work. He always vowed he composed from the head in preference to the heart, but in spite of himself, the fusion is magnificently achieved. I recall the sagacity and analytical perception of Lewis Mumford; Lewellyn Powys' poetic acceptance of life's indifference to man; the impersonality of Shakespeare who celebrated the actions and reactions of *all* men and whose wisdom had a Biblical determination; the laconic lessons of T.S. Eliot; the innovative thinking of D.H. Lawrence and his extra sensitive responses to all things, both material and spiritual; the masterly control of the word-image in the poetry of Christopher Brennan and the depth of his probe into classical mythology; Norman Lindsay's once radical slogans from his book *Creative Effort*, 1924, always stimulated me in my revolt against the status-quo. I closely noted his literary efforts and even today I think he wrote with more discernment and judgement than he ever revealed on canvas. And who could but love the poignancy of Rupert Brooke:

'Oh never a doubt but somewhere I shall wake
And give what's left of love again and make
New friends, now strangers...
But the best I've known
Stays here and changes, breaks, grows old, is blown
About the winds of the world and fades from brains
of living men and dies.

Nothing remains.'

Life today is manipulated by the photographer behind his camera. Magazines, newspapers, advertising, junk mail, television, coffee table books, posters, X rays, medical photography—all affect our subconscious with directions to do this, buy that or think something different. Only a few stalwart minds can fight off these attacks on our hard-won individualism. But there is another kind of photography, proportionately minuscule, which induces delight, spiritual harmony, an abundance of emotional excitement and intellectual wonder. By some strange coincidence it is said to be related to art, but those who do the relating cannot define art so the final classification never really materialises. I for one do not wish to see photography propped up by an affiliation with any other graphic method of expression. It is unique in its own right and must be kept that way! Photography of this calibre is still embryonic and its inherent direction is only just being discovered. It is to be seen hung in public galleries, in private collectors' portfolios and in

MAX DUPAIN, 1938
This was taken by Olive Cotton at Longueville, Sydney.

the storage cupboards of individual photographers. It is the kind of photography which requires words like 'esoteric' and 'personal initiation' to describe it. It often derives from the photographer who has turned his back on life and seeks solace and satisfaction in his own consciousness. It has no connection with the run-of-the-mill junk photography used in the boring daily round of a consumer society.

A flight of thought suggests that the forces working within current photographic parameters will create an aesthetic front of a new order with new relationships and new values between man and his environment, a kind of 'immaculate perception' which could help clarify man's understanding of himself.

Towns and cities

CIRCULAR QUAY SCENE, CIRCA 1950s
The Indonesian trading ship, Dewarutji, *is parked at the old wharf, Circular Quay. She sailed through the heads with white, billowing sails—a beautiful sight. The AMP building on the right is nearing completion—it was to be the tallest building in Sydney for some time.*

SHIPS, DARLING HARBOUR, 1941
A view slightly north of my Clarence Street studio shows morning activity on the wharves.

SYDNEY, 1938
Overleaf: Early morning view from the south pylon of the Harbour Bridge which was then the highest point in Sydney. There is no smog, and beautiful early morning light rakes the city. An exhilarating visual experience.

COLLINS STREET, MELBOURNE, 1946
This photograph was one of the highlights of a big propaganda exercise about Australia's way of life directed at potential migrants. All the capital cities and environs were included.

STREET AT CENTRAL STATION, 1938
Early morning scene at Central Railway Station, Sydney. It was one of many pictures taken to fulfil a commission for a book called Soul of a City, *published by Oswald Ziegler.*

COLLINS STREET, 1946
This is the Paris end of Collins Street, Melbourne. All very charming, with a flavour reminiscent of many boulevards in Paris. Now demolished in the name of material progress.

SALAMANCA PLACE, HOBART, 1946
Beautiful old store buildings characteristic of much architecture in Hobart. I think they have been mostly demolished. This was photographed mid-morning with a storm brewing in the background over Mount Wellington.

COUNCIL WORKER, 1938
A foggy morning in Hyde Park. This council worker is cleaning up the park before the day begins. His pipe suggests the tempo of the day.

GEORGE STREET SILHOUETTE, 1935
One of the last hansom cabs on another foggy autumn morning, this time in George Street, Sydney.

CIRCULAR QUAY, CIRCA 1960s
This picture was taken from the old Harbour Trust building, now demolished. It features the construction of the Quay railway with the old Macquarie Street stores in the background, also now demolished.

VIEW FROM CLARENCE STREET STUDIO, 1947
*Storm brewing over the old berthing facilities for international
tourist liners, with the old brick buildings and wharves of
Victorian vintage in the foreground.*

CIRCULAR QUAY, 1938
As a ferry passenger, I frequented Circular Quay regularly. In those days I carried a camera all the time and this picture was seized on my way to work.

SYDNEY HARBOUR CREPSCULE, 1937
This scene was photographed from the south pylon of the Sydney Harbour Bridge on a very still autumn evening. An exposure duration of about 15 minutes allowed the ferry lights to register their travel paths across the film.

BACKYARD, BARROW CREEK, 1942
This is a reminder of the first taste of cold chicken and moderate temperatures since leaving Alice Springs several days before. Our hosts entertained us in an underground cellar which was refreshingly cool. Up above it would be 35° and dry as dust.

BACKYARD, FORSTER, 1940
Washing day seen from my hotel window. This intimate urban scene was taken during a trip through the Central and Northern Coast of New South Wales in my old Chevrolet Roadster.

SMOKO, SALAMANCA PLACE, HOBART, 1946
Council worker and his horse take a break in front of the ships'
chandlers and general stores. Since then, the machine has
completely altered life in Hobart—as everywhere else. Horse
and cart are now redundant.

SUMMER DAY, KINGS CROSS, 1938
These were the days when Sydney had a population of just over
a million, which is evident in the relatively deserted streets.
This is Darlinghurst Road in summer, at noon, and it's hot.

INTERIOR, SYDNEY UNIVERSITY, CIRCA 1950s
I had intended to create a book illustrating life in context at the university. Hundreds of exposures were made but the finance to publish was not forthcoming. The architectural connotation of this picture particularly appealed to me.

TWILIGHT, SYDNEY, FROM AWA TOWER, CIRCA 1960s
This was then the highest viewpoint in Sydney. Now it is difficult to find among the skyscrapers. I have long been interested in night-time photography. Darkness fulfils my eternal quest for simplicity by enveloping unnecessary detail. Mystery prevails.

MONA VALE LANDSCAPE, 1936
An image comprising land and people which has a surreal quality. It is an optical puzzle. These situations are around us all the time; it is for us to observe them if we wish to enrich our lives visually.

NUNS IN A CITY STREET, 1937
It is hard not to be affected visually by the beautiful silhouette of a nun's garb. When I go out on architectural jobs, I often wish I had some nuns in the kit!

LINER AT NIGHT, 1940
I used to go out looking for pictures at night and I came upon this liner at Woolloomooloo. In an experimental way I made several exposures of various durations and finally came up with this one. It looks simple, but technically it taught me a great deal about the control of light by correllating exposure and development.

ALFRED STREET, NORTH SYDNEY BY NIGHT, CIRCA 1940s
This is a technically more sophisticated picture than 'Liner at Night'. The difference is due to long exposure and what is termed 'soft development', so the contrasting material of bright lights and dark context is minimised by way of underdevelopment. I discovered that the time for night photography of this nature was almost exactly half an hour after sunset at any time of the year in the Sydney area.

NEW AND OLD, 1936
This is a story of contrasts. The almost Renaissance form of the cross is silhouetted against what was then admired as modern architecture in Bligh Street, Sydney.

MELBOURNE FROM ST PATRICK'S, 1946
I waited a long time for the shadow to move into the centre of the left-hand spire to indicate the existence of a third spire. It is interesting to note in the background the building height limits.

PADDY'S MARKET, 1938
An early morning scene which could be witnessed any day of the week as suburban shopkeepers purchased their wares from wholesalers. Buying and selling activity was intense.

CLOSE-UP AT PADDY'S MARKET, 1938
Here is a woman truly doing a man's work. I cannot remember seeing this happen at any other time at Paddy's.

PLAYTIME IN WOOLLOOMOOLOO, CIRCA 1950S
Life begins in the street for these children. To dwell on the problem of kids living on the street means confronting all the problems of contemporary urban society. For these kids the street is their playground.

COUNTRY PUB, JERRYS PLAINS, 1942
A typical timber country pub in New South Wales, with galvanised tank, pitched roof and wide verandahs. It couldn't be anything else but a pub in rural Australia. It is being cleaned up for the day's trading.

PEAK HOUR, NORTH TERRACE, 1946
When Arnold Haskell landed in Australia with the Ballet Russe in 1938, one of the first things he said was, 'I immediately fell in love—with Adelaide.' This handsome garden city would be hard to resist in any of its moods. Even rush hour looks like a pleasant Sunday afternoon in Sydney.

MOONLIGHT, CIRCULAR QUAY, CIRCA 1947
Light has always had a fascination for me and is a major seducer, day and night. In this picture I am shooting into the light which silhouettes and automatically simplifies the total form of all objects involved.

KINGSFORD-SMITH SOUTHERN CROSS, 1947
This is a trial flight of the restored aircraft over Federal Parliament House, Canberra.

NORFOLK ISLAND, 1985
A long shot looking towards Kingston illustrating the restored old buildings. The work was directed by architect Philip Cox & Partners. Philip spent the best part of 16 years on this project.

BROOMS FOR SALE, CIRCA 1940s
I came across this display on a main street in a Sydney suburb.
I went in to inquire about the price because I needed a broom,
but there was not a soul in sight.

MORNING, KINGS CROSS, CIRCA 1935
The era of the ice chest, when you had to leave an enamel basin
on the front step to receive your daily delivery of an ice block.
The refrigerator did not become common until much later.

EIGHT FOR SIXPENCE, 1936
*Street barrow in the Eastern Suburbs, Sydney. A choosy
customer picks out her fruit.*

CROWS NEST FRUIT MARKET, 1950
It is interesting to compare price tags then and now. The presentation of fruit and vegetables remains the same though, as do the people.

ARTHUR CIRCUS, BATTERY POINT, HOBART, 1946
This consisted of about 20 houses built around a circle of lawn (like the old village green), inhabited by the upper class soldier of the day and other government employees.

OLD DOLLS RESPRAYED, 1955
At this stage of my development I was very interested in a documentary approach to photography. This window in Clarence Street is an attractive example of documentary material because of the singularity of its contents.

THE SHOW SEASON, CIRCA 1940s
A man digs in his pocket so that he can buy the last balloon of the day at the Royal Easter Show, Sydney.

HOBART SIESTA, 1947
This was the scene every day of the week at lunchtime in Franklin Place. It is indicative of the pace of life in the 1940s. Oh, nostalgia!

BOOKSHOP IN BOND STREET, 1935
Friday, late-night shopping in Bond Street, Sydney. Gilmore's Bookshop was located very near my first studio. The shop was run by a German refugee who would visit the studio frequently with the latest haul of photographic books from Europe—most of which I still possess.

RUSH HOUR IN KINGS CROSS, 1938
I was with Damien Parer when I took this photograph. He had relatives with a flat above this intersection. No exposure metres were available in those days so the light had to be assessed by experience. With the primitive Rolleiflex, exposure time would be approximately one tenth of a second at full aperture. Note the movement of the vehicles in the foreground, whereas in the middle distance they are foreshortened enough to show no movement at all.

MARTIN PLACE FROM THE BANK OF NSW, 1938
Flower and fruit stalls used to decorate Martin Place before it became a pedestrian mall. The clock tower was removed the following year when war broke out, and was not put back until after the war.

MARTIN PLACE BY NIGHT, 1939
This is the tranquil Martin Place of the 1930s where some of Australia's largest companies established their offices. It was the most prestigious address in Sydney. Now it no longer has the same air of elegance.

HOBART WATERFRONT, 1947
This little harbour is usually a hive of activity for all kinds of vessels—fishing boats, interstate ships, private yachts. This happened to be a Sunday morning when everybody was still in bed. Some of Hobart's famous architecture forms the background. On the left it is being replaced by steel and concrete.

THE OLD SPIT BRIDGE, MIDDLE HARBOUR, 1935
The first drawbridge over the Spit. It replaced the vehicular ferry which connected north and south points. The show boat is about to pass through. Clontarf and the beginning of Sydney Harbour form the background.

MOSMAN BAY AT DUSK, 1937
This technique is similar to the one used in 'Sydney Harbour crepscule', page 35. This scene by day would be comparatively uninteresting but at twilight, when so much detail is subdued and artificial light takes over, an element of romance and mystery becomes evident. This is highlighted by the 'spaghetti' line of the Mosman Ferry.

TWILIGHT, PEAK HOUR, SYDNEY HARBOUR BRIDGE, 1946
A complex rendition of moving car lights across the Harbour Bridge. This was taken from the top of the southern pylon with a lengthy exposure to show up all the 'spaghetti'.

CENTRAL STATION, 1939
Sydney was still relying on trams. You can imagine the discomfort one had to endure by simply looking at them! They were poorly sprung and noisy—a most unsophisticated system of travel.

STREET SCENE, HOBART, CIRCA 1946
This illustrates an even more primitive version of the Sydney tram, with the exposed open deck aloft. It was just after the war and servicemen were still visible in the streets.

THE NATIONAL BANK, CIRCA 1940s
Photographed in the main street of a country town. This bank was not open for business—the 'staff' were probably out at lunch, or maybe there was a race meeting!

EURELLA RAIL STATION, 1979, NORTHERN QUEENSLAND
I was photographing CSR's recently-acquired cattle stations when I happened upon this weird edifice out in the sticks. How often the trains connected with this station I do not know, but it wasn't often!

BERRIMA, 1941
One of the oldest towns in New South Wales—a little oasis— with a pub claiming to be the oldest. The Berrima jail and courthouse are both architectural landmarks: the latter is a museum piece and the old jail has been converted to a reform school for prisoners. Almost all the fine old buildings of Berrima have been restored under the direction of architects and are open for public inspection.

NINE MILE STORE, MONA VALE, EARLY 1930s
This was a popular general store at the time. Proceeding north, the next stores were in Newport, Avalon and Palm Beach. The population was pretty sparse and the general stores few and far between. This one operated on the main highway, Barrenjoey Road. General stores sold anything from lawn-mowers to cigarettes.

PERTH, 1945
One of the main streets of Perth. It exhibits all the order and stability which impressed me in this beautiful city.

ST. JAMES' CHURCH, KING STREET, EARLY 1940s
St James was designed by Francis Greenway who also designed the adjacent Supreme Court which was restored by the Public Works Department several years ago. This is the hub of some of the finest Georgian architecture in Australia including Hyde Park Barracks, the Mint Building and Old Parliament House.

TRAM ABSTRACTION, CIRCA 1930s
Exposed mid-morning from the T&G building in Park Street, Sydney. This photograph was taken into the light which reflects into the steel rails to form a geometric pattern.

CENTRAL STATION, SYDNEY, 1939
If there is such a thing as tram nostalgia, here it is! This was one of the main terminals for trams which then proceeded into the city and out to the suburbs as far as Abbotsford, North-bridge, Watsons Bay etc.

PEOPLE

BANKSTOWN BOYS DON'T CRY, 1942
But one has a runny nose! An 'in passing' shot taken during my time at the camouflage school in Bankstown.

LITTLE AUSSIE, 1942
I saw him by a railway crossing. He was watching for the odd train and opening the gates for cars to cross the line. He stayed that way while I stopped the car, got out and took his picture.

MARITIME COMMUTERS, CIRCA 1950S
Early birds on their way to work, having disembarked from the Manly Ferry, Curl Curl. *This was a re-take for the 2nd edition of Oswald Ziegler's* Soul of a City.

BONDI, 1939
This group represents what Picasso used to call 'found things'. It occured spontaneously, during a sunbaking session, never to be seen again.

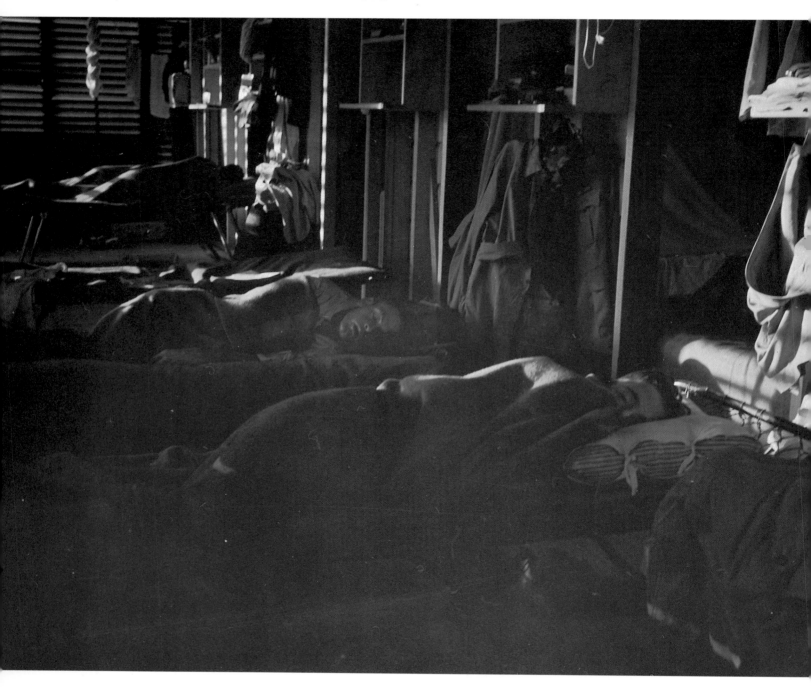

SLEEPING RAAF PILOTS, CAIRNS, 1943
Pilots billeted in what was once a private house, photographed early in the morning after returning from a 'milk run' Catalina bombing raid on islands north of Australia. They would depart Cairns at dusk and return to base at dawn—exhausted and ready for bed.

RAAF CONCERTINA PLAYER, CAIRNS, 1943
Airforce man off duty, practising for a concert. This was taken in Cairns when the RAAF were stationed there during the war.

PETTYS HOTEL, SYDNEY, 6 PM, 1941
*This pub was at the corner of Clarence and Jamison Streets.
The time was known as the 'six o'clock swill', since pubs were
forced to close at that time. It was the alleged reason for so
much drunkenness after work hours.*

JESUS EVER LIVETH, 1940
*This picture was taken in a charity organisation, the Sydney
Rescue Society for destitute men, women and children. The foreground figure was embarrassed at being photographed and
turned away from the camera. It was a novelty for the kid.*

OUT OF WORK, 1938
Photographed in Sydney Domain during the latter part of the Depression. I paid him 10 shillings as a model fee and on receiving it he headed straight for the pub.

DOMAIN DOSSER, 1938
This character was genuine. He had slept the night under the rocks with scant clothing. He managed to raise a toothless smile at the invitation to be photographed.

MOTHER AND CHILD, 1952
My wife Diana and daughter Danina (an Aboriginal word meaning 'to bid farewell') at Toowoon Bay on the Central Coast of New South Wales. My wife is catching up on sleep having been awake during the night with her teething daughter.

DIANA, 1941
An early portrait of my wife taken in the Clarence Street studio. It was made on a paper negative which consists of a negative made on specially thin paper from a transparent positive image of the original negative. Simple!

LITTLE GIRL IN A THUNDERSTORM, CIRCA 1950s
This evolved from a professional assignment to photograph a client's children. During the session a sudden storm blew up, with thunder and lightning followed by a rainbow. The child was perplexed and anxious and I managed to catch her that way.

BLACK AND WHITE IN CAIRNS, QUEENSLAND, CIRCA 1960s
I photographed this prettily dressed and well cared for Aboriginal child on my way to a sugar mill during a commission for CSR. I was jokingly upraided by my slavedriver companion from CSR for wasting the firm's time!

HALIFAX, QUEENSLAND, CIRCA 1960s
Halifax is a sleepy town—one horse, one pub. Quite spontaneously this door suddenly enclosed a group of three, curiously eyeing the photographer. They watched in leisurely style, propped up against the wall in typical Queensland manner.

REFUGEES AT THE SYDNEY RESCUE SOCIETY, CIRCA 1950s
Prayer time at a charity organisation. The society cared for people of all ages from all walks of life. This group performed for the camera and the seriousness inevitably went out of prayer.

FASHION PHOTOGRAPH OF THE 1930s
This typifies the glamour period which I endured in the early stages of my development. It was all about creating a make-believe atmosphere. The silhouette in dress suit and top hat is a rear projection onto a glass screen.

NORMAN LINDSAY, 1936
The grand old man of Australian art: painter, etcher, supreme pen-draughtsman, ship model maker, writer, genius. A radical thinker, his essays in affirmation were intellectual succour for the students and thinkers of his day. He wrote novels, philo-sophical treaties and exhibited a versatility which was un-matched by his contemporaries.

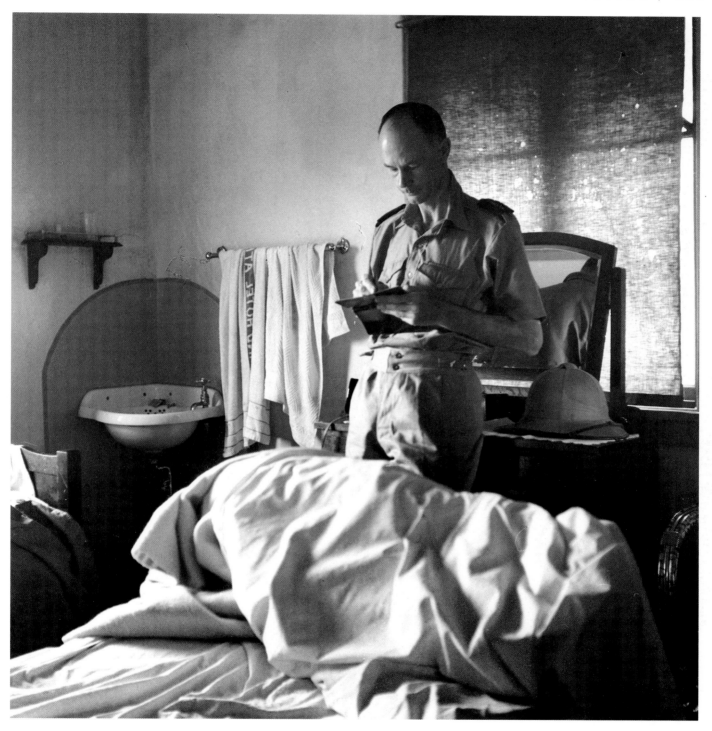

OFF-BEAT, 1960
*George Street, Sydney. This was part of a 'Life in the City'
series for the book* Soul of a City. *The leasureliness of the
period is expressed in the subjects' faces.*

ROBERT EMERSON CURTIS, 1943
*I worked with Bob who was a commanding officer of
camouflage during the war. We were based in hot, steamy
Cairns. When we arrived at Atherton, still in shorts and shirts,
we froze near to death. Bob was a prolific diary keeper and here
he is hard at work in our hotel bedroom before breakfast.*

SIGHTSEERS IN A BUS, CIRCA 1950
When the Caltex oil refinery opened at Kurnell, buses were made available for curious visitors. I had covered the total construction progress of this installation with Kerry Dundas and this was one of the winding-up shots of the commission.

AT THE SHOW, 1960
Most photographers were inspired by Cartier-Bresson's dictum about the 'decisive moment', and by his fascination for life more than photography. This is one of my 'decisive moments'. The purpose of the long stick of rolled-up newspaper carried by the man on the right remains a mystery.

SUNBAKER, 1937
Previous page: The sculptural form and weightiness of this figure has become a life symbol for many Australians for whom sun, sea, the beach and the body are synonymous.

PORTRAIT OF A BOY IN SUNLIGHT, 1936
Taken on a beach, this is a good example of the use of soft sunlight in the making of a portrait. The luminosity of the shadows has been effected by reflected light from the beach.

THE GRAMMAR EIGHT, CIRCA 1940s
I rowed for Sydney Grammar in 1929 and 1930. We got nowhere, but it was one of the highlights of my school career. Oarsmanship cultivated self-discipline, teamwork and school

patriotism. This crew is taking off from the pontoon at Gladesville, watched anxiously by the coach.

THE LITTLE NUDE, 1938
The nude figure, like the portrait, is one of the most difficult subjects. The nude requires great simplification of its complex form and I have attempted to achieve this here.

TIRED SOLDIER IN TRAIN, QUEENSLAND, 1943
This picture was taken near Kuranda in a primitive train on the way back to Cairns from Atherton. It was a long, rambling journey during which everyone slept at one time or another.

RUSSELL DRYSDALE, CIRCA 1960s
Artists make great material for photographers because of the character of their studios: well-used palettes, brushes, bottles, rolls of paper, canvases in stacks, and usually a very congenial and sympathetic person to deal with. 'Tas' was no exception.

LLOYD REES, 1979
Another interesting studio. Lloyd didn't like his picture being taken, declaring that he froze up at the crucial moment. I think he was being overly self-critical. Nevertheless, the expression of concentrated scrutiny on his face indicates the throes of visual analysis—and for the moment nothing else matters.

CURIOUS BOY, CIRCA 1970s
Belgian photographer Leonard Misonne once stated: 'Le sujet n'est rien, la lumière c'est tout', (the subject is nothing, the light is everything). In this photograph, the light from the horizon merging into the dark sky of Northern Queensland and the boy slashed with low level light, investigating the mechanical complexities of a farm implement, could not be passed over.

FRANCIS LYMBURNER, 1941
Just as photographers carry cameras Francis always carried a sketch book and pen, and a great part of his leisure time was spent drawing friends in context. He is doing just this during a picnic at Bungan Beach.

COOLAH LANDSCAPE, 1959

Very often, viewing a scene from a car is deceptive. When one parks the car and investigates the subject there is, for some unknown reason, a breakdown in the imagery. This, however, is an exceptional case. I was taught at art school that the foreground is the most important part of a picture. The strong silhouette of the tramp and the shadow cast by low raking light lends acute perspective and pictorial importance to this otherwise solitary landscape.

BUS QUEUE, THE SPIT, 1946
We had more patience then than we have now! The camouflage-patterned bus indicates that this was just after the war, when even in Australia people were glad to come by most things, even if they had to queue for it. These people wait with wartime patience for a city-bound bus.

GRAFTON JACARANDA FESTIVAL, CIRCA 1950s
I am inevitably seduced by black, and these silhouettes of old ladies, with the whimsical elderly character in the foreground, just had to be photographed. The focal point, of course, is the craggy hand grasping the bag.

WOMEN AT A WEDDING, CIRCA 1940s
Grand old ladies having a chat. This was another 'decisive moment', where character meets character and their conversation fills the air. It is supposed to be a joyous occasion!

LUNCH BREAK, WORKERS OF THE WORLD, CIRCA 1940s
A gathering of builders' labourers at a factory site in the Western Suburbs. This picture is about making the most of what you have in a dark, cavernous enclosure. It had to be taken by flash for adequate luminosity.

FOOTBALL MATCH, SYDNEY OVAL, CIRCA 1950s
Reading from left to right: hope, despair, disbelief, dis-
approval, smugness, dissatisfaction and neutrality (the law).
It takes all types to make a football audience.

SMILING BOY AT GLEBE, 1939

He was a beaut boy. His father had just left for the war and I was commissioned by his mother to make some family pictures of them both to send to her husband at the front. I have never forgotten these happy people.

ROY DALGARNO, 1943

Early portrait taken in Darwin during the war. Roy was politically oriented towards the left and the arguments which rent the air during our encampment were very lively. Since then, he has established himself as a well-known painter and exhibits his work regularly.

THE QUEEN, 1954

When the Queen visited Australia in 1954 most people were determined to see the newly-crowned monarch. The most popular section of the royal route was Macquarie Street and it turned into a gigantic hotel overnight. Hundreds of people slept there, ate there and established their chosen positions in order to get the best view. They suffered great discomfort, it was hot and humid but they stuck it out for hours and hours until the Queen arrived. I guess the total viewing period would have amounted to about five minutes. How mad can you get?

THE QUEEN, 1954
Activities were numerous during the Queen's visit. There was a brisk business in the sale of souvenirs, flags, ice creams and fast food. The crowd was made up of all types, all shapes and sizes, some bored, some elated, some doing their duty, some wondering what it was all about. Kodak did a roaring trade!

HOT DAY, ROMA, QUEENSLAND, 1980
The bottle tree (baobab) lines the streets of Roma. Its intri-
guing shape is a great visual stimulant. These two Australians,
exhausted by life and heat, make a marvellous compliment to
the volume and texture of this extraordinary organic form.

STOCKYARD, NORTH QUEENSLAND, 1980
Heat and dust and frantic activity in a CSR cattle station. I
am always amazed at the fearlessness of cattlemen. They have a
way of intimidating these animals which can be so ferocious in
a mob.

AIRPORT SCENE, SYDNEY, 1938
*This was Kingsford-Smith Airport in the early stages. It was
not complicated enough to be disorganised!*

REX'S FIRST WATERFALL, 1960
*Children's holidays at Minnamurra Falls, NSW. The
avalanche of falling water caught the imagination of my
son Rex. Wonder and alarm about falling water filled his
conversation for days afterwards.*

ELEANOR DARK, CIRCA 1940s
I photographed this famous Australian author for Ure Smith.
A senstive writer of historical fiction including
The Timeless Land *and* The Storm of Time. *During the*
sitting she was quite matter of fact and cooperative, but she
didn't like it very much.

BILL DOBELL, 1942
One of Australia's most famous portrait painters. He was
knighted towards the end of his career. At the beginning of the
war Bill volunteered for the camouflage corps. He is photo-
graphed here in the design office at Bankstown airport which
was a major camouflage training school.

LAND AND SEA

NAUTILUS, 1954
This was not a 'found thing', but a conscious organisation of available rocks at Pebbly Beach, NSW, and a nautilus shell from Sydney. The scene was lit by low sunlight.

TOOWOON BAY, CENTRAL COAST, NSW, 1985
My intention was to photograph this cowry shell in a rock setting when suddenly figures appeared. So I withdrew the viewpoint and achieved what I consider to be my best shot of 1985.

KARRI FOREST, PEMBERTON, WEST AUSTRALIA, 1945
This is a land of skyscraper trees which dwarf the individual in scale just as city buildings do. This picture was taken when the felling of trees was still done by axes and crosscut saws, before the chainsaw was introduced.

BLUE GUM FOREST, GROSE VALLEY, NSW, CIRCA 1940s
Early morning with the bushwalkers. Sunlight streams through the smoke from the bracken fire which was lit to achieve this effect.

MAGNOLIA, 1982

This is one of the most beautiful forms. It is complex in its natural state and I have endeavoured to reduce this complexity to a simple statement with the use of a single light and a symmetrical viewpoint.

AUSTRALIAN WARATAH, 1967

The flower form is one of my pictorial addictions. In this close-up we have the vibrant colour and the remarkable structure of the waratah. It was photographed in the wild in bright sunlight.

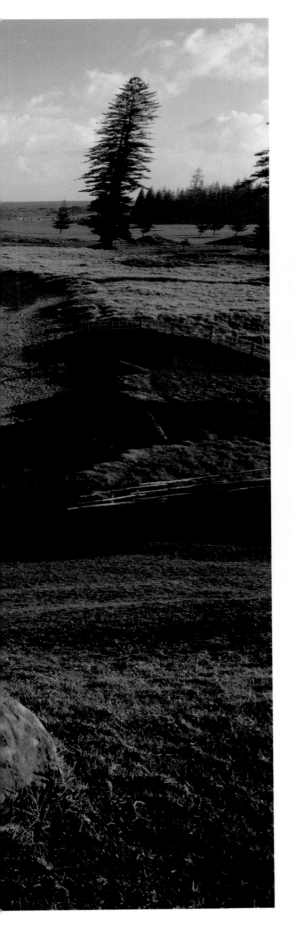

SANDSTONE CAVE AT GLENORIE, NSW, 1983
This is a cave in the 'backyard' belonging to Sidney Ball, the painter. I happened to be photographing his house which was designed by Glenn Murcutt and I discovered the cave in a search for viewpoints. Aborigines had been here. We introduced hand shadows to intensify the mystery.

NORFOLK ISLAND SEASCAPE, 1985
I love this seascape, so wild and untouched by human hand. As an urban dweller it satisfies my craving for the organic. My only feeling is that colour photography has made this too real. It does not have the latitude for interpretation like black and white photography, and in my view mere mechanical depiction is inadequate.

SEED PODS ON THE WARATAH, 1967

The form and colour of the waratah when it goes to seed is in muted contrast to the flower, but the character remains the same. The hard flower produces a hard pod—linear in form as opposed to chunky like the flower.

THE WILD NIGHT, CASTLECRAG, 1984

A still life combination of Hawaiin lilies with a timber sculpture by Bim Hilder, photographed in the twilight. This is one of a series of flower forms which begins with the lily and is followed by the firewheel tree flower, camellias, waratahs etc.

BARGES ON THE CLARENCE RIVER, NSW, CIRCA 1950s
Empty CSR cane barges about to take off for the fields for the transportation of cane to the mills.

CANE CUTTER, INNISFAIL, QUEENSLAND, CIRCA 1950s
This was taken when cane cutting was done by hand, mostly by Italians. Slashing cane with a blade was a very arduous task, rarely undertaken by Australians.

SURF RACE START, MANLY, CIRCA 1940s
Actions like this have to be anticipated; in this case by me standing out in the surf with camera and waiting for the start. One shot only—I had to be lucky and I was.

TAKING IT EASY, BONDI, CIRCA 1940s
Any Saturday afternoon, even today, you can witness this characteristic Australian pose. The bell is a shark alarm— not for the sharks, for the surfers!

SOUTH WEST ROCKS, 1978
One of the few isolated beaches on the North Coast of New South Wales. It is beautifully unspoilt, serene and wild. The beach is practically always empty. There is no feeling quite like the exhilaration of walking along a deserted beach.

STANWELL PARK, NSW, LATE 1940s
The beauty of the South Coast of New South Wales was un-rivalled until civilised man moved in.

MCCARR'S CREEK, SYDNEY, CIRCA 1970s
I prize this shot as one of my best exhibition pieces. A tiny portion of desolated land, my interpretation has converted it to a mysterious setting by virtue of the black overtones and fragments of scattered highlights.

SEASCAPE BY NIGHT, 1980
One of a series of pictures which illustrates the life of a Norfolk Island pine tree over a period of seven years. Beginning with the flourishing young tree, it ends with bare bones and death. This stage was photographed by moonlight at the Newport cottage.

WARATAHS AND THE MOON, 1983
The waratah grows in sand, needs little water and will endure acute changes in climatic conditions—except floods.

FLOWER OF THE FIREWHEEL TREE, 1983
Nearly all the flower pictures were taken at night with introduced artificial light and sometimes available light.

'HERO' TOWING OUT THE 'PAMIR', CIRCA 1940s
Unfurling of the sails began at Circular Quay and by the time we reached the Heads the ship was fully furled. It presented a magnificent sight with the light south-wester filling her sails.

MANLY FERRY HOLIDAY TIME, CIRCA 1940s
One of the largest Manly ferries filled with animated people on their way to a harbour celebration. This shot was taken from another ferry passing alarmingly close.

NIGHT LANDSCAPE, CASTLECRAG, CIRCA 1970s
Concurrently with the flower series I became interested in the landscape at night, lit by artificial light. This gigantic rock with angophora tree forms part of my wild garden.

CASTLECRAG LANDSCAPE, CIRCA 1970s
A little park which was rescued from oblivion by local residents assisted by the local council. This was taken in the height of summer when the flannel flower sings its loudest.

MANLY BEACH, CIRCA 1940S
Photographed from the shark observation tower, now demolished. Heights have always excited me. This viewpoint *opens out the subject material, extends the pattern potential and avoids confusion caused by overlap, as from eyelevel.*

AT NEWPORT, 1952
I made several rapid exposures of this scene as the lad

*began to climb out of the baths. I wound up with this
linear, sculptural form—the luck of anticipation.*

SOUVENIR OF FRENCH'S FOREST, 1939
The fascination of rock forms with delineating shadows is one of the strong attractions of the bush for me. It comes under the category of 'discovered images in passing'.

WALLABIES IN A BANKSTOWN BACKYARD, 1942
A chance shot of tame young wallabies frolicking in a domestic environment. The back lighting was fortunate—it emphasises different textures.

SOUTH AUSTRALIAN LANDSCAPE, 1946
The Adelaide hills are a delight. Undulating and neatly kept orchards, vegetable gardens and crops make a colourful patchwork garment of the landscape. Neat and ordered old-world German villages introduce a refreshing European flavour.

LATE AFTERNOON PASTORAL, 1932
One of the last sentimental shots of my 'pictorial' period. Taken in what was then the Mona Vale wilderness and is now a residential suburb.

MANLY, CIRCA 1940s

This is how I used to spend my weekends, taking pictures for exhibition as a break from commercial work. This is another shot taken from the shark observation tower of the launching of the surf boat, observed by Sunday spectators.

'MORNA', 1938

One of the largest and most elegant yachts on Sydney harbour —always a wonderful sight. It is not difficult to imagine the excitement experienced when the Manly Ferry I was travelling on overtook this beautiful yacht which was beating to windward into a north-easter.

STANDLEY'S CHASM, ALICE SPRINGS, 1943
The scale of this vast chasm in the MacDonnell Ranges has the same impact as Ayers Rock. I walked though the red granite pass where white sapling eucalypts spurt out of the rock. These rock formations arch into a cobalt blue sky.

AYERS ROCK, 1985
An unforgettable experience is to move in close to this vast monolith and sense the intense drama. This low view increases the elevation and the form is accentuated by the slashing light raking the textures.

GLOUCESTER LANDSCAPE, NSW, 1951
This is a pictorial school derivative, brought up to date by modern optics and ancillary materials. It also expresses drama, emphasised by the central highlight on the land and the dark silhouette of the background mountain.

APPROACHING STORM AT TOOWOON BAY, NSW, 1951
Even on holidays the camera is indispensable. On this particular afternoon walk the landscape was transformed by a violent storm approaching. It caused light to shoot dramatically through dense cloud. This picture has a threatening mood which appeals to my sense of theatre.

BUNGAN BEACH, NSW, 1931
*A deserted beach and a delight to the eye. It is now no longer
deserted due to a housing development which has been built in
the vicinity. Shame.*

LOWER PORTLAND, 1931
The tranquil water on the tributary of the Hawkesbury River has a therapeutic effect. Both this photograph and the one on the previous page were taken with primitive equipment in the shape of a vest pocket Kodak. When they were enlarged, the enlarger was also primitive enough to burn a gas mantle as the light source.

LOG HUT, CIRCA 1930s
Probably once a homestead and now a shed in need of restoration, somewhere in New South Wales. One of the old style buildings, architect unknown, now gradually disappearing from the land.

ROADSIDE STORE, CIRCA 1940s
A vegetable store near Camden, New South Wales, run by PT Morton ex AIF. This used to be a common scene on Australian highways, and most of the produce was locally grown.

ALICE SPRINGS LANDSCAPE, 1943
White gums sprouting out of red granite in dry heat on the edge of a dried-up river bed. The Alice Springs pictures were all taken during a fortunate delay in a wartime journey to the Darwin camouflage headquarters.

ALICE SPRINGS LANDSCAPE, 1943
The dry bed of the Todd River. The flourishing white gums, with their roots well submerged in the subsoil, are surviving in this dry state until the next rains come.

SOUVENIR OF HAGLEY, 1947
One of the most common rural scenes of my first trip to Tasmania. The peaceful atmosphere typifies the ease of life in the apple isle.

NORFOLK ISLAND LANDSCAPE, 1970
Another organic tranquilliser. The atmosphere of Norfolk Island is similar to that of Tasmania, although the structure is different is so far as the landscape is undulating and there is not the same amount of rural activity. Serious photography begins with the large format camera. The Norfolk Island series was taken on 5 × 4 film.

FRENCH'S FOREST WATERFALL, CIRCA 1940S
*Heavy rain in the spring has produced an avalanche of water
which will dry up very quickly after the rain ceases. This was
taken during a clearing in the cloud.*

SUNDAY AFTERNOON, MANLY, 1950
A classic weekend afternoon at Manly in the height of summer.
It is all pattern punctuated by figures in motion. Notice how the
high viewpoint 'opens out' the panorama.

PRAWNING AT THE ENTRANCE, NSW, CIRCA 1950s
During the prawn season, after dark, those who relish that delectable morsel gather at the lakeside and wade into the prawns with their nets of all shapes and sizes. I experienced this, as well as the supper that followed. Delicious!

THE JETTY, SILVER BEACH, NSW, 1952
I was all set to photograph this jetty near Kurnell for fun, because of its steep perspective and silhouette appeal of the little shed at the end, when in walked this little girl with a barrow and made my day.

LANDSCAPE AT NIGHT, CASTLECRAG, 1979
Unless striving for movement I prefer dead still nights for this type of photography so that the variety of textures is not smudged. This shot was lit by one 500 watt floodlight, and some of the exposures extended for five minutes.

THE BLUEBERRY ASH FLOWER AT NIGHT, 1984
The blueberry ash flower, enlarged to thrice its normal size. Delightfully delicate in structure and a wonderful decoration for the magnificent tree which bears it. Like most native flora it is totally scentless.

AT WARRIEWOOD, SYDNEY, CIRCA 1950s
The wind blows from the west and breaking waves become
combers. The variety of textures which the camera can render is
one of the factors which makes the daylight picture supreme.
Here we have waves breaking over seaworn rocks, with the soft
smooth texture of human flesh in the foreground.

THE FLOATER, CIRCA 1940s
*Many of my pictures are taken quite spontaneously, and this one
is no exception. Photographed in the Northwood Baths, it has
an essence of calmness and peace.*

Papua new guinea

NATIVE WOMAN, 1943

Nadzab was one of the areas we worked in as camouflage officers during World War II. I came across this woman with child in a native encampment during an inspection trip of some of the camouflage areas. She is dressed in the typical traditional Christian way—the missionaries had been at work.

NEW GUINEA LANDSCAPE, 1943

Camouflage headquarters were on Goodenough Island and the RAAF mess hall was some distance from our camp. This happened to be a morning landscape on the way to breakfast. It looks cool and serene but it was hot and humid.

STAND-DOWN DAY, 1943
This day was generally a Sunday and the boys and girls took to boats and ploughed through the not very turbulent waters of Port Moresby Bay. Compared with the northern zones, Moresby was reasonably civilised.

NIMADAO RIVER, NEW GUINEA, 1943
We were camped on a hill above this river. The water was crystal clear, except after rain. It was a beaut place for bathing and washing clothes, and the sound of it sent you to sleep at night. These boys are RAAF troops on a washing spree.

NATIVE GROUP, GOODENOUGH ISLAND, 1943
The natives were intrigued by the camera which is evident from their facial expressions. When they started approaching I became a bit anxious, but their seeming enmity was mere curiosity.

DESERTED NATIVE HUTS, MOUNT NIMADAO, 1943
This was 900 m (300 ft) up Mount Nimadao. Several of us decided to climb up as far as we could one Saturday afternoon and this is a souvenir of that trip.

ARCHITECTURE

JAMBEROO HOUSE BY GLENN MURCUTT, 1985
This is intended to symbolise Glenn Murcutt's system which involves corrugated iron cladding and the principle of air conditioning by reticulation. This is evidenced in the separation of levels in the main roof to induce air convection.

EL ALAMEIN FOUNTAIN, KINGS CROSS, 1968
A machine-made interpretation of the dandelion. A brilliant idea, designed and executed with consummate skill by Robert Woodward. I photographed it at night because the artificial illumination gives maximum reflection from the steel stamens which are not as obvious in daylight.

FRAGMENT, ST PETER'S CHURCH RICHMOND, 1962
Built in 1841 and designed by Francis Clarke. An example of sandstock brick technique, beautiful executed.

ST MATTHEW'S, WINDSOR, NSW, 1963
Considered to be Francis Greenway's masterpiece. St Matthew's was built in 1817 of sandstock brick and has been kept in good repair since it was recognised as a building of great value. A porch was added in the 1850s on the southern side, and the shingle roof has been replaced with copper.

PORTICO, OLD GOVERNMENT HOUSE, PARRAMATTA, 1963
The graceful portico, doorway and fanlight were designed by
Francis Greenway. Much of the building dates from 1815, the
architect being John Watts, the military engineer. It is now a
showpiece open for public inspection.

FRAGMENT OF THE SYDNEY OPERA HOUSE BY NIGHT, 1968
Architecture and the night photograph are complimentary
because I believe the mystery of architecture can well be
intensified at night.

NEWMED HOSPITAL, NEWCASTLE, NSW, 1984
Designed by Lawrence Nield & Partners, this is a fine hospital which suggests the breakaway movement in post modern architecture, where form does not necessarily follow function.

HOUSING COMPLEX, QUEENSLAND, 1985
A modern group of houses designed by Harry Seidler & Associates which is much more in the Bauhaus tradition than the building in the last photograph. The foreground consists of a decorative pergola which fronts onto the swimming pool. The pattern created by the foreground gives relief from the austere form of the housing complex.

YULARA TOURIST CENTRE, 1985
This resort was designed by Philip Cox as a self-contained village intended to encourage tourists to visit Ayers Rock. It comprises an international hotel, a visitors' centre, civic centre, retail and community areas, school, campgrounds and recreation facilities. This is a close-up of the polyester sails which are sunshades for the podium.

THE FOYER OF NEW PARLIAMENT HOUSE, SYDNEY, 1985
This beautiful fountain designed by Robert Woodward is the focal point of the foyer designed by the Public Works Department. In the background is a series of my Georgian architecture photographs.

CSR DEMOLITION, O'CONNELL STREET, SYDNEY, 1962
Regrettably, the stairway went the same way as the pillars, cornices, wrought-iron lifts etc. I was told that to incorporate the stairway within the new building would have cost in the region of £1000 and the idea was rejected on that account.

STAIR RAIL, ANZ COMPUTER CENTRE, 1975
The form of this modern stairway designed by Joseland & Gilling is sculptural in essence. It represents the aesthetic entering the commercial field.

SUBIACO, 1962
The stately Doric columns carved out of one piece of stone are unique in Australian architectural heritage. When the building was later demolished to make way for a factory, the columns were donated to the University of New South Wales. They were re-erected there in the same format as the original design.

THE CUPOLA, ELIZABETH BAY HOUSE, 1980
This wonderful mansion designed by John Verge, and restored by Clive Lucas has a famous stairway, pictured here, which embraces the interior of the dome. It is one of the most sophisticated examples of Georgian architecture in Australia, and a delight to photograph. It is open to the public.

SYDNEY OPERA HOUSE BY MOONLIGHT, CIRCA 1970s
One of the final shots in a series depicting the building of the Opera House right from stage one. It amounts to about 1000 negatives. This was not a commission, but a labour of love.

ROSS BRIDGE, TASMANIA, 1962
Designed in 1831 by John Lee Archer, a Tasmanian colonial architect, this bridge was completed in 1836. Even though it was built for vehicular traffic which constituted a few horses and carts, it now carries all kinds of motor vehicles which it was not designed to carry.

BROWNLOW HILL, COBBITTY, NSW, 1980
A charming country house built in 1828, probably by John Verge. It was the country home of Alexander Macleay whose town residence was Elizabeth Bay House, Sydney—also designed by John Verge. Brownlow Hill has one of the most outstanding colonial gardens still flourishing.

INTERIOR, GLENFIELD, NEAR CASULA, NSW, 1960
Photographed for the National Trust, this interior belongs to one of the smaller Georgian houses which I photographed for Georgian Architecture in Australia. It was built in about 1817 by Dr Charles Throsby and has since undergone total restoration.

THE ROUND TOWER GUARDHOUSE, PORT ARTHUR, TASMANIA, CIRCA 1940s

A wonderful example of early colonial architecture, built in 1835. Beneath the building were cells for convicts awaiting transportation to Hobart for execution. Restoration has been prolific since this picture was taken, yet it is impossible to be here without feeling abhorrence for the abject cruelty which was perpetrated by the British on their fellow men.

THE FLOUR MILL, KINGSTON, NORFOLK ISLAND, 1970
Norfolk presents historically a more melancholy scene than Port Arthur. Total incorrigibles were sent to Norfolk and treated accordingly. This building contained a treadmill where convicts were forced to work 12 hours a day grinding grain. It has since been restored by Philip Cox & Partners.

YULARA TOURIST CENTRE, 1984
*A super wide-angle abstraction of the support structure for
solar screens over part of the podium. The white polythene sails
(see page 198) float above so that the effect of the direct sun is
minimised. Summer temperatures can reach well above 40°C.
Designed by Philip Cox.*

MID CITY CENTRE, SYDNEY, 1982
*The form of the barrel vault became the trend in Australia in
the late 1970s. This was one of the first and largest. Designed
by Harry Seidler & Associates, this shopping mall is still
classified as smart and elegant.*

INDUSTRIAL

CSR RIG, 1984
*Early morning in the Simpson Desert, Northern Territory.
This oil rig is silhouetted against the brilliant red sky which
matches the red land beneath it. The air is cool and dry but by
11 o'clock the temperature will be up in the nineties. The mulga
scrub in the foreground struggles for life.*

BAUXITE PILE, ALUMINA, 1970s
Alumina stockpile in tropical Queensland, near Gladstone. The conveyor belt arm feeds the bauxite from the processor to build up this stockpile. It is one of the many industrial landscapes which are now common in Queensland's wildernesses.

INDUSTRIAL SCENE, CIRCA 1960s
An illustration of the use of coloured lights to increase the pictorial intensity of what could otherwise be a drab scene.

OXO PLANT, CSR CHEMICALS, CIRCA 1970s
Another example of the machine form lending itself to photographic treatment. Taken on a still night to increase the intensity, I would call this a good example of colour photography as the colour is muted, not garish. This chemical plant is on the tributary to the Parramatta River.

BAUXITE BINS, QUEENSLAND ALUMINA, CIRCA 1970s
With major industrial installations, the photographer can be sure of drama on tap. I chose a low viewpoint for this photograph to increase the vertical perspective.

MCWILLIAMS WINERY, GRIFFITH, 1962
The wine industry now uses stainless steel storage vats which take on the contemporary image of the machine, as in other industries. Here, an operator is hosing down one of the vats to reduce the temperature.

NEWCASTLE WATERFRONT, 1947
Huge Australian hardwood logs being loaded for transport overseas.

TUMUT, NSW, 1973
This is good example of form following function. These huge, steel water pipes inch their way over the landscape supplying water to the power stations in the area. Note the scale illustrated by the figure in the foreground.

MAURICE O'SHEA'S MOUNT PLEASANT WINERY, HUNTER VALLEY, NSW, CIRCA 1940s
This old-fashioned screw press used for white grapes only is being operated manually. It would be hard to find this scene today in the vineyards since all the crushing is now mechanised.

MINERS DRILLING, 1947
Miners in the bowels of the earth drilling at the face. One has to visit a coalmine to realise how arduous the work is and what a singular life these men lead. By the nature of their work environment they are a race apart.

LOADING BAUXITE, WEIPA, NORTHERN TERRITORY, 1963
This almost Wagnerian scene taken in the heat of a tropical night had all the drama of an opera. The thunderstorm on the left of the picture reinforced this impression.

HARDBOARD FACTORY, TUMUT, NSW, 1977
Overleaf: Industrial form is such a fascinating subject. The camera has an affinity with the machine and machine-made products. A product of the 20th century, the camera is a machine/instrument like any other—for making pictures.